Flacofolio

FLACOFOLIO

Micro-Essays
by
Leonard Schwartz

—

Assemblages
by
Heide Hatry

spuyten duyvil
2025

Published by Spuyten Duyvil
www.spuytenduyvil.net

All artworks are produced and photographed by Heide Hatry
in 2024 in NYC, one block from Central Park.
Design and layout by Heide Hatry.

ISBN: 978-1-963908-54-1
Library of Congress Control Number: 2024952162

Excerpts from this book appeared in the fall issue of *Cable
Street* as well as in *The Brooklyn Rail*.

Cover image: *Flaco 2012-2024*, *Icons in Ash* portrait, made
from the bones of Flaco's prey.

For Flaco
and all New Yorkers
who loved him

Table of Contents

Wikipedia

Flaco (March 15, 2010 – February 23, 2024) was a male Eurasian eagle-owl who escaped his long-time enclosure at Central Park Zoo in New York City after someone cut the protective netting in February 2023. Flaco subsequently resided in and around Central Park. His escape attracted significant public and press attention, especially as he was of a species not native to North America. There were concerns for his ability to feed himself after being captive for so long, since he had not needed to fly or hunt, but he was seen successfully catching and eating rats a week after his escape. Attempts to recapture Flaco failed, and a petition circulated advocating that he remain free. Zoo officials ceased attempts to recapture him once it became clear he was eating on a regular basis and his flying skills improved.

Though he was able to hunt, there were lingering concerns about potential dangers in the park, like rodenticide. He remained in Central Park for nine months, eventually wandering to nearby buildings and neighborhoods in Lower Manhattan. In February 2024, one year after his escape, Flaco died after colliding with a building on Manhattan's Upper West Side.

Eagle-Owl I

The death of an eagle-owl ends up meaning something to millions. Other such small deaths proceed amidst the enormity, unrecorded. Certain types of animals, including our type, scavenge for the absolute. One stands in for many.

Owl II

People attempt to cheat death one of three ways: belief in an after-life: the having of children: making a work of art to guarantee presence. Then there is the eagle-owl dealing out death to rats and pigeons, itself dying violently in the strange.

The Death of Flaco

The raven is the bird Poe associated with the an-
nouncement of Death. Did a raven appear before
the eagle-owl's greatest admirer to announce the
accident that very night? Which ornithologist
predicted the inevitable the most clearly, well be-
fore? Exactly how many died during Covid before
the eagle-owl broke from the memory of banging
pots and pans to offer the city a new conceit, a
hero, a narrative contra confinement? We are all
erotic animals. That's what makes his death so
terrible.

The Tragedy of the Eagle-Owl I

Certain raw truths rip open the personification. But fiction matters too. The life of a lone owl and a proliferating virus may seem opposite ends of a spectrum, but each posits both the truth and the fiction, just as rat poison accumulates in creatures beyond the rat. Nor are the circumspect and the sudden mutually exclusive. The tragedy of the owl builds from the circumstantial to the immediate.

February 2nd, 2023

The eagle-owl escaped in winter, on February 2nd to be exact. The burning lanterns of his eyes perhaps kept him warm throughout the first few nights and days. The soul does not remain in the world it was sent to.

March 2023

Arboreal no island, escape is partial. The lanterns of his eyes catch the remaining sunlight, at night the sunlight reflected from the moon.

The soul, sad to say, remains in the world it was sent to.

The eagle-owl, an elsewhere, now is here.

"The collapse of contemporary societies comes from the ugliness of what we have built."

– Joseph Brodsky

Flaco landed on a windowsill and peered in at the couple that lived in that particular apartment.

A City Far from Eurasia

To know a hunger deeper than the flesh of rats and pigeons. To be a universe unto oneself when one would prefer to be a part. To hoot of it throughout the night without real hope of answering calls.

Storm

Just the way treetops and tree roots splay through their respective elements, sensing some soon coming gale, I never fall asleep at night but surge instead through the darkness. Though the idea of home is a fiction, I have never felt so much a part of anything as I do this coming storm. During this part of my flight Blue turns into Night.

The Tragedy of the Eagle-Owl II

The English word "tragedy" comes from the ancient Greek "tragos oide", meaning "goat song". No one knows exactly why the Greeks linked "goat" to the tragic, though it might be due to the bleating a goat makes before sacrifice or slaughter.

Now NYC must reflect on the relationship between "goat song" and "owl song". What does "owl song" mean, if the goats at the Central Park Children's Zoo seem cheerful enough?

Some of those goats have wattles.

Years ago I made up a word for my daughter to refer to "goat wattles". That word was "scotchy".

Now we have the proper noun "Flaco". Perhaps his soul continued, past the glass window.

Scapegoat

During the pandemic there was a great deal of toxic individuality on display nationally about business closings, wearing masks, staying six feet apart, and the like. New Yorkers were more disciplined than that, having seen death up close at the beginning. Later there was an unconscious desire for Flaco at least to be free from all constraints, from all protections in his name. But he got poisoned out there. Owl song is indeed haunting. One shouldn't be didactic.

No Exaggeration

For thousands of years the eagle-owl had to deal with the cruelty of its captors. Then, for a decade, it had to deal with the capriciousness of its liberator. Who was it that let the eagle-owl out? It isn't known. Though in fact the bird knew only a little over one year of liberty.

Time and Space

In old age I plan to join the migrating geese. The prospect of a return migration should be enough to keep me young. But many owls aren't built to migrate. And new worlds can be harsh for even the largest of them.

Ecology I

Ideas about the "Third Landscape" abound. This is the idea that "nature" and "city" now overlap to create a new space. A crack in the pavement in Chelsea plays host to wisps of vegetation and some ants. Central Park becomes a home for racoons, coyotes, hawks, owls, and even, for a little over a year, a Eurasian eagle-owl. The 19th century European landscape painting values of "urban", suburban", and "rural" may no longer suffice. Flaco suffered in the indecision as to whether they do or not.

Ecology II

Ants don't care if it is Chelsea or Washington Heights across whose sidewalk and sidewalk-cracks they scuttle or parade. Yet there is nothing "natural" about Flaco's presence. Out of step, out of wing, but adapting, adapting...

New and unexpected circumstances greet us all. "Eco" means "home", but it isn't clear what "home" means. Flaco refreshed the grounds of perception and in the richness of the specialized feathers covering his breast and head the city itself fought back against its own deficiencies.

Driftwood

Driftwood is sacred. The eagle-owl was that. Hatched in North Carolina, shipped to the Central Park Zoo. Liberated, he resided in Manhattan, like many other displaced beings before him. And a message in a bottle, pitched into the ocean, is also driftwood…

"Being a phenomenon of language, the poem can be in its essence dialogical, a message sent out in a bottle – certainly in the not-always hopeful belief that somewhere, sometime it will be washed onto land, into heartland perhaps. This is how poems travel: oriented towards something; towards something that stands open, that can be occupied, perhaps towards a Thou that can be spoken to, a reality that can be addressed. A poem, I think, is about such realities".

– Paul Celan

The City I

The city had been through a lot, and the liberated eagle-owl offered a new start, a way out of Covid and confinement. The way that the eagle-owl died gave the outward appearance he wanted back in, into the warmth of the human fold. The fact is we have no idea what the bird did or did not want. We barely can make out what we want ourselves. Sometimes we do make out what we want and the contradiction hurts. A cognitive cage is a cognitive cage.

Circulation of the Song

A heart with a beak.

A heart with eyes, epidermis, feathers, wings, and a beak.

A heart and other organs with a mind and a beak and an outlook.

A heart with a beak.

Ontological Consideration

Have you considered the idea that the eagle-owl might have been the ghost of an ancestor, haunting the city? Or else, an ancestor reincarnated? In the latter case of which, now that the eagle-owl has crashed and died, he must be incarnate elsewhere. A snow leopard cub near Mustang, the youngest of three in a frisky brood. The progeny of a Belgian couple that fight too much. A lonely desert poplar, its thin trunk barely sticking out from above the sand.

Or, if he was a ghost all along, perhaps he has now simply slipped out of being altogether.

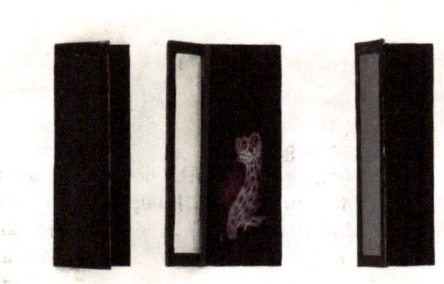

Proximity to the Penguin House I

During his captivity the eagle-owl attracted solitaries, poets, teenagers in angst. However deep their dreams the *flaneur* and the *flaneuse* found their way to Flaco's enclosure at the Zoo, just outside the exit from the Penguin House. A visitor went from a crowd of noisy, social, gentoo, chinstrap and king penguins, a large crowd of people gathered in front of their frosty glass divider, to Flaco's tiny coop outside that house, in the warm or bracing air, depending on the season, separated from people only by the wire. Many people never even noticed the eagle-owl.

Proximity to the Penguin House II

The penguins stood around, their chests thrown out, diving into the water and swimming about, their squawks, live or recorded, broadcast into the House, mingling with the excited sounds of children and parents, all stepping up to watch them. Just outside the exit to their House the owl sat silently in his cage, one eye occasionally opening to match your gaze. Who is to say it wasn't one of those solitaries or poets that scaled the wiring to snip open the mesh on top and free the owl? Can a book solve a mystery?

Two Beings

The lightning is fashioned anew, even speedier than before, even further out in front of the sound, more slanted, more electric. Summer came to the city, a giant bolt bisecting the darkening blue. The young woman and the eagle-owl might as well have been the only beings in the emptied Park; drawn together, they feel the peril, they await the thunderclap that surely follows. The lightning bolt illuminates each for the other.

Phenomenology of Flaco

The mind learns to bracket certain questions and some overpowering emotions. Once bracketed the thing that the questions and the emotions would have obscured can be seen. That something isn't necessarily real. The questions and the emotions had reality too. The clearly seen is a supreme fiction. Yet the owl seems to look back at me from the safety of a limb and be the very embodiment of a concrete encounter with reality. The clear imprint such Being leaves on consciousness – consciousness, which is empty and non-substantial – offers the mind a kind of Being, despite everything.

night   bird

flight

still   sacred

quiet

swift-winged

strife and battle   minds

in sleep

in   waking hours

lie

with pain,

Sweep

There is something sad about the individuated. It locks us into a particular place, a specific station. Individuation of course also can bring a sparkle to things. But one sees the sadness of it on the face of a kid on a train platform, a kid not going anywhere, perhaps having just said goodbye to a family member that boarded the train.

The kid must stay behind, in an obscure suburb on an obscure shore that in and of itself seems abashed about itself. Whereas there is something about the word "Eurasian" that speaks of a grand sweep, a colossal span of wings. "Flaco" is individuating, but it is also a trap. The cage of a name a creature carries with it, the creature itself majestic and forlorn, as it were completely individuated…

Out at Night

From inside a beauty that attracts male suggestion as to what should happen next, from the inside of the scent of a flower, that focusing attention of a sexual receptivity in all its sensory forms, for which the eagle-owl cries, having already consumed his fill of rats and pigeons for the night…

Whodunit I

A young woman makes it a point to regularly visit the eagle owl in his cell. Release the male from his terrible confinement? Little Red Riding Hood might not have necessarily preferred it to be the wolf waiting in the bed for her – his electric fur, the hunger in his eyes; she might well have preferred her grandmother, I suppose. Her grandmother! A fluffy owl on the other hand... his need to be helped... those big blinking eyes... the intentness of their gaze... his wings spreading over her bosom...

Whodunit II

Once upon a time a young woman regularly visited a caged eagle-owl with thoughts of freeing it.

I'm not saying that I know who freed the owl. I would never say that.

Anyhow, it must have been the man that liberated the male from such confinement, right?

The Man

The man imagined a time without condoms, without AIDS, without concern about any venereal diseases, a time when presumably nobody cared who was impregnated by whom. His was a tale that was going to get very messy. But it felt good to tell it, like liberating an eagle-owl from the constraints of a very tiny coop without worry about any of the consequences. Surprisingly, the city went wild for his story. Or maybe it isn't so surprising.

No Obvious Exorcism

Ever since my birth, my birth has possessed me. It guides my every move. I cannot think apart from my emerging from the egg, for which there is no obvious exorcism. Ecstatic, rising above myself, no longer myself, in flight through night's prolongation, silent, winged, free...but still ravenous (ravenous!), still desirous (filled by a joyous burning emptiness), still unsettled. Every living being desires to wander and change. New York City is a world.

Eclipse

He wonders where his life lies. First there was total confinement, then there was total liberty. "I saw the totality in Tennessee in 2017", a passerby says, referring to an eclipse. On the threshold between winter and spring, during the 90% eclipse in 2024 in New York City, the streets were filled with people looking skyward, many wearing funny looking cardboard glasses. On East 18th Street a random guy lent me his welding glass, of which he was proud, and looking through it I could see the moon cut in front of the sun as if a few feet away.

This was 45 days after the eclipse of the eagle-owl, by which I mean the death of Flaco, and 46 days after Flaco had wondered where his life lay.

Earthquake

On the threshold between winter and spring there was also an earthquake in town. That is something one rarely experiences in New York. I felt it off 116th Street – and pretended to myself the shaking came from construction next door. But my body knew it was an earthquake. It told me so, even as my mind pretended otherwise and was the winner in the moment, till informed otherwise. The mind and the body often tell us something different from each other about the same thing. This was the case with the liberation of the eagle -owl.

The Waterbirds are on Alert

The waterbirds are on alert. Each is universal and each is particular. The fish are on alert. Each is universal, each particular. Do Jersey's marshlands tempt the Eurasian eagle-owl to fly across the Hudson? And what of the further continent beyond, rolling all the way to Colorado, to California? What keeps the eagle-owl in the city?

City II

One bitter cold winter in Beijing I saw some 40 owls perching in four trees in the courtyard of a Confucian temple. In normal conditions these owls don't flock. But cities produce unusual circumstances for many kinds of creatures, including owls.

City III

A black lizard, camouflaged in the obsidian: it is invisible. When it darts it is visible for a moment, all nervousness, all nerve. Somewhere in the city's reaches lies this shrine ensconced in obsidian, and this black lizard is its god, worshipped in the stone, only occasionally glimpsed. Sometimes people can find the animal in the inanimate, the god in the animal. Religious passions are intense. They are brief in the absence of an institution to frame them and often aren't even noticed.

Then There is This

The spiritual is unobservable. The city is soaked in the unobservable, despite all the cameras. An owl and an octopus are observable, are observable and unobservable, are open and closed. The one without the bones – that would be the octopus – lives deep in the sea, or on display in an aquarium. The one that throws up little packets of bones, rather than excreting feces, is often high up in the trees. Those are the owls, one of which was Flaco. The octopus has eight tentacles because the seventh day is the day of rest, and on the eighth day you return to the work. Thus, the octopus is always beginning, beginning again and again, as in the writings of Gertrude Stein. But there is no agreement about the telos of the eagle-owl. Creation is a chameleon.

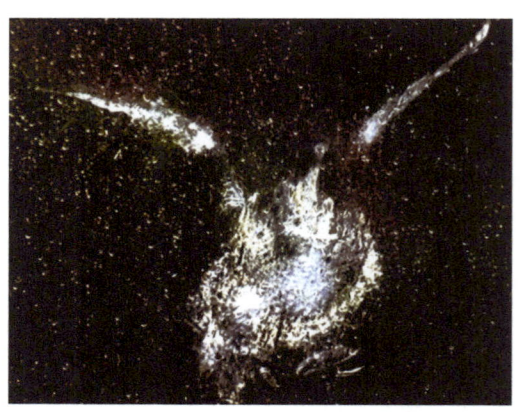

Flacoseries

The explorer Henry Hudson believed the river that would eventually bear his name would ultimately lead him to China, not to Canada. In 2000, 2001, and 2002 the director Peter Hutton made a film about the two rivers the Hudson and the Yangtze, joining them together, as in Hudson's dream. Hutton filmed the Yangtze just as certain towns were being flooded for the dam and certain cliffs were collapsing. He filmed the Hudson in the winter when it was ice. The two rivers are thus connected in the imagination. A Eurasian eagle-owl is part of this imaginary, leading right out onto the steppes and Central Asia as much as he does to Europe.

Size

The "eagle" in "eagle-owl" presumably refers to the impressive size of the owl. Heide saw the shadow of his wingspan in the moonlight one night in the park and it was indeed impressive. Could the "eagle" in the name have also suffused Flaco with a whiff of US nationalism? Can we imagine the eagle-owl eating rabbits like an eagle? When an eagle is part of the name of an owl the possibility of the hybrid is in play, just as with "Eurasian". "Flaco" is most commonly a Latin American name. There it means "skinny."

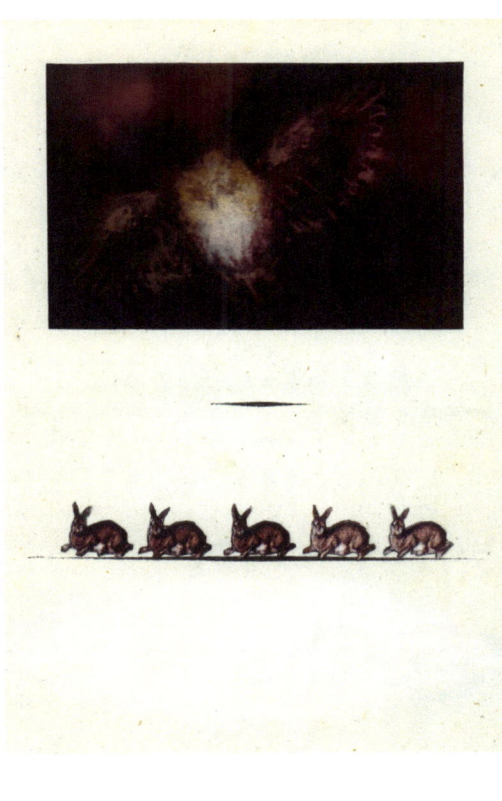

Favorite Oak Tree I

St. Leonard is the patron saint of prisoners. St. Francis delivered sermons to the birds. The Persian poet Attar wrote an epic called *The Conference of the Birds*. Pasolini offered us a Marxist crow. Flaco is related to all of them. There was a memorial erected around his favorite oak tree to roost in, in the northern reaches of Central Park. There is a petition circulating to create a statue of him at that spot. The message of any such shrine… will have to be determined. There are multiple possibilities.

Favorite Oak Tree II

The northern end of Central Park, though certainly not deserted, is wilder than further south. I would have guessed Flaco's favorite perch would be off CPW and 103rd. But it wasn't. It was on the eastside of the Park, near 104th, not far from what I call the secret garden. Devotees of the eagle-owl – birdwatchers, seekers after a tie to Nature, concerned citizens – created a temporary memorial to him there after his death. The offerings were varied: flowers, notes, stuffed animals, cards. What is the appropriate offering to make to the memory of an owl?

Rumi's Father

"Ecstatic people are not critical of others."
— Bahauddin, *The Drowned Book*

Flaco was not critical of others. Not only did the owl bear everything with dignity, he thrummed with Being. What to say about the question of his personhood? May we speak here of the ecstatic? What is the appropriate offering to make to the memory of an owl?

Rhyme Prose

"Body and breath do a turn together", according to the owl in Chia Yi's rhyme prose from the Sung Dynasty. The rest of the time body and breath are separated, body lying someplace one way, breath flying somewhere else like a draft. "The rest of the time" is to say so much of the time it is almost all. How fortunate to be in this city then, where body and breath seem to overcome nonbeing on a regular basis, and with such an unusual energy! An owl is both an ill omen and a strike against obscurity. Silken feathers and sharpened talons go both ways.

Bird Sighting,
Lincoln Center Reflecting Pool

"Heaven is overrated: there is nothing there."
– the wife's ghost in Apichatpong's film
Uncle Boonme Who Can Recall
His Previous Lives

Rain drops hit the surface of the reflecting pool. The ancestors cannot be deep down there since the water is so shallow.

A thin sheen disturbed by the downpour: the perfect place for a large bird to drink standing in the water in the quiet and the mist of earliest morning...

(At the zoo Flaco barely vocalized. At large in the city, he cried out nearly every night.)

(Quiet again, but not tranquilized by its new condition, after the crash.) (Flaco blinks, the poem is in the blinking.)

Relatives

It seems that in ancient Egypt some relatives of the eagle-owl were treated violently while alive because birds of ill omen, sometimes even decapitated, then mummified and deified after their deaths, to serve as important psychopomps. Perhaps Flaco's soul did continue past the glass window his body imprinted on during the fatal collision. The soul does not remain in the world to which it was assigned.

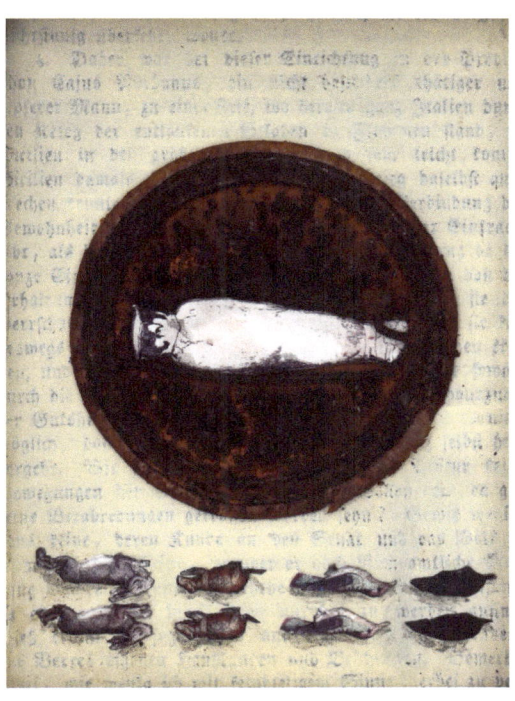

Dream

A cage of fire dangles over the limo's dashboard. The limo isn't exactly part of a funeral procession, but it is a part of a related transmigration. Several of us seem to be going. Indeed, a Akwesasne Mohawk friend had warned me not to spend too much time talking with others about owls.

Between the cage of fire and the encircling fog, it is hard to see much of anything out the front windshield.

From the Lower East Side
to the Northern Reaches of Central Park

The classicist Jane Harrison wrote of "the spoken correlative of the active rite". The rite might involve a chariot. It might involve a pilgrimage. It might involve an owl. Anselm spoke of bringing his family uptown to look for Flaco, after Flaco had visited the Lower East Side but they had missed him, and that he and Karen were more overwhelmed than the kids when they did see Flaco in the Park.

Shut Eye

"Let's pretend we are two owls napping", the fatigued father said to his son, "you can be the owlet". In this way the father could close his eyes for a few moments and flirt with sleep. Indeed, a few seconds was all it took for the sleeping owlet to turn back into an energetic boy. The trance of the self is rarely broken. The human mind is closer to the mind of an owl than it is to a computer.

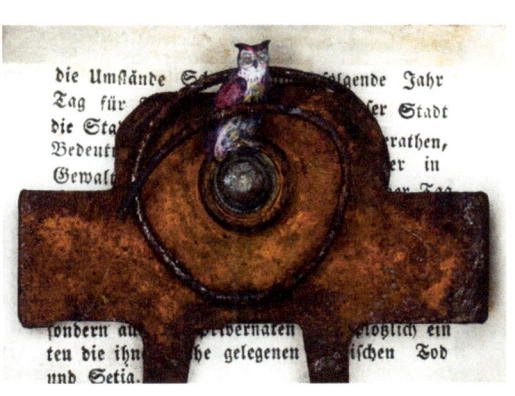

Squirrel I

I saw a crushed squirrel on the curb on Hudson Street, near the Bus Stop Café. It had obviously been run over by a car, or by a bus. Streaked with blood and uneven pulp, inner organs pressed to the surface, it was nonetheless recognizably still a squirrel. Immediately I thought of the eagle-owl. News reports only spoke of rats and pigeons as the objects of his hunt, but surely squirrels too could be prey. To identify with the bird and his needs, and not the squirrel, so much biologically closer to me, shows how fully Flaco allowed us to overcome our mammalian bias.

Squirrel II

There is a genre called "roadkill poetry", in which the writer reflects on the meaning of a dead animal on the side of the highway. Somehow this scenario doesn't fit the circumstance of the squirrel squashed on the curb near the Bus Stop Cafe. The death of this squirrel seemed more dignified, the corpse less "roadkill" than the body of a fellow pedestrian, something one could identify with, as opposed to identifying with the car or the bus.

This empathy was only overridden by the fact that I immediately thought of the eagle-owl's hunger. I wondered if he could eat the dead squirrel. I hoped he might put in an appearance in the neighborhood and find it there at night, even though owls are not generally thought of as scavengers.

Writing

I wound myself around the wheel of the chariot like rattan and in this way assisted in transporting the god. I allowed myself to be lifted up and carried away by the eagle-owl and in this manner helped to feed him. I flung myself into language.

Fana

Fana is a word in Sufi mysticism that refers to the annihilation and overcoming of the self. Years ago, an artist from Wuhan painted a huge bird on the wall of a building on 8th Street between 1st and A, a bird that appears to be holding its own feathers and skin, which are gripped in its talons and dangle downwards as the new incarnation of itself soars through the air. For four years I have referred to this bird as the *Fana* bird, fiercely carrying off the remains of its own former life. Now there are murals to Flaco spray-painted all over the city. These are testimonials to self and other.

...iese Thiere, eben so leicht wie ... ist als für, — auf ihre ...lucht auch die Unverwundeten mit fort. Nun warf nicht ...loß ein Banner, sondern jeder Krieger für sich. Wer nu ...amme die stehende Elephantenschaar erreichen konnte, ...pieße auf dieselbe. Um so eiliger rannten die Thiere un ...ie eigenen Leut, und machten noch weit mehr, als sie unt ...u Feinden gethan. Also nieder, weil die Gewalt des ...em Thiere sitzenden Lenkers ... dachte viel schwächer ist ...ie Furcht, welche es ... Schrecken gesetzt fortschen ...u die von dem Thiere ... und verwirrte Li ...rangen die Römischen ... und brachten die B ...heilten und Bestürzten nach kurzem Widerstande zur Flu ...jetzt ließ Marcellus auf die Fliehenden die Reiterei einha ...d die Verfolgung hörte nicht eher auf als bis sie zittern ...r Lager getrieben waren. Denn außer so Vielen, was ... ...en und verwirren mußte, waren auch noch zwei Elephanten ...mitten im Thore niedergestürzt und die Feinde sahen sich ge ...öthigt, über Graben und Wall in ihr Lager zu springen ...ier wurde das größte Blutbad unter ihnen ... gerichtet; ...en achttausend Mann wurden getödtet, ... fünf Elephanten

Central Park

New Yorkers dream of Central Park as a space in which all classes mingle and people and plants co-exist, with other species too. But Central Park is no Mecca for random animals. Liberal cosmopolitanism is the only answer, but ultimately it too failed to find a place for Flaco.

Self and Other

There are murals of Flaco spraypainted all over the city. On the Bowery near Stanton on a wooden board that is part of a business's façade is a painting of Flaco's head, only the head, bright red against a background as yellow as his eyes, his eyes and beak central, black and white tears that might also be feathers shedding to each side of his face. Near Houston Street a giant multicolored Flaco towers over a rendering of the city's skyline, a blue snake slithering rightwards above the owl's head. Coming up from the subway on 2nd Avenue is a cross eyed Flaco with "King Flaco RIP" spraypainted in black over a blue background under the tuft of his left ear.

The testimonials are to eye contact. To I and You. To the expressivity of the face without expression. To the expression not of the personality but the soul.

Attar's "The Conference of the Birds"

"The owl came forward with a bewildered air and said: I have chosen for my dwelling a ruined and tumbledown house. I was born among the ruins and there I take my delight – but not in drinking wine. I know hundreds of habited places, but some are in a state of confusion and others in a state of hatred. He who wishes to live in peace must go to the ruins, as the madmen do. If I mope among them, it is because of hidden treasure."

– Attar, as told by Elizabeth Gray

After Attar

"Like a crazy, I have shed the lived in places, chosen ruins. For the silence. For those moments when the nameless dead remove the talismans and you can sense the blue dome-fragment in the household wall."

> – Elizabeth Gray, "The Owl Declines to Accompany the Other Birds on Their Quest for The Divine Simurgh"

From the Beginning

From the beginning I so hoped the eagle-owl could make it out there, on his own.

Boat Basin

The French *nouvelle vague* director Jacques Rivette made a film, *Celine and Julie Go Boating*. At the end of the movie, after many hours of delightful mystery and confusion, the two titular ladies do in fact finally go boating. On the water Celine and Julie encounter the ghosts and otherworldly beings they have interacted with throughout the film, who silently paddle by them in their own boat, in pursuit of some unknown end, members of neither craft acknowledging the other by word or sign.

Is this the way we encounter Flaco, visible but in some parallel world, from behind a film of incomprehension, perhaps the incomprehensible itself? One can do this kind of boating in Central Park.

Spring

In Istanbul there is a spring sacred to Apollo. Around that spring is built a Christian chapel. Around that chapel is built a mosque. The spring of water itself is the simplest magic, and it is discovered last. The eagle-owl is a reminder of it. "Angel" comes from Greek *angelos*, meaning "messenger".

Requiem for Flaco

Flaco was not an idea, he was an actual bird. The owl at the goddess of wisdom Athena's side was some other owl and not this one. Our ideas gather around the eagle-owl like crows mobbing a bald eagle. Eventually the eagle flees and perches on the far palisade.

Flaco Receives a Full Necropsy

When the knife cuts into the corpse, the dead body gives way, and surrenders up pieces of itself, until it is nothing. When one living body cuts across another living body in lovemaking, there is a surrender of another kind. It is certain the eagle-owl's body knew the first, all absence. In love, one surrenders oneself wholly to presence. Perhaps Flaco did know love like that in some way we cannot sense.

Full Necropsy II
(Kill the Messenger)

The lovemaking body plunges into its counterpart and wraps it up, keeps it warm, entangles itself there, vanishing as a particular entity, while the pathologist's hands plunge coldly into the dissected body, transforming it into unmediated matter. A knife peels away layer after layer of emotion. Can the artist find even more than the pathologist in the very meat of the animal? The necropsy uncovered three different types of rat poison. "Angel", from Latin *angelus*, means "messenger", as I've previously mentioned.

Flacoseries

*To be full of being and yet completely empty: that
has been my circumstance from the start. My iden-
tity, now as ever, is where I'm not. Just as soon as I
have conquered the whole city, I know I don't belong
there; mounting the tower I plunge into mourning.
Heaven and earth are waterfalls tumbling in me
and also hints of something and somewhere else.
Coop and cosmos can and cannot contain me.*

The New York Times

May 28, 2024

Partial remains of Flaco, the Eurasian eagle-owl whose escape from the Central Park Zoo and year on the loose enthralled New York City before his death in February, will be kept at a museum near where he spent most of his life, zoo officials said on Tuesday.

Flaco's wings and tissue samples have been transferred to the American Museum of Natural History, where they will become part of the scientific collections, according to a statement from the Wildlife Conservation Society, which operates the Central Park Zoo.

On the Nature
of Things

List of Images

Heide Hatry and Flaco the Owl, what a perfect couple. Hatry has also escaped from her artworld cage and what better tribute to nature's brave non-human souls than her witty and heartfelt assemblages. — Lucy R. Lippard

All images included in *Flacofolio* are details of unique artist's books created by Heide Hatry in New York City in 2024, one block from Central Park. Hatry visited Flaco often and had a number of powerful and intimate experiences with him, some of which resulted in receiving gifts, in the form of his pellets, which she has integrated into a few of the works represented here. Most of the present assemblages are incorporated into excavated, century-old books.

In Between. Assemblage with text by Siri Hustvedt printed on mycelium and painted paper cutout.
5.4 x 4.4 x 1.25"   21

Schatten des Todes I. Sculptural assemblage with rusted sheets and rag paper figure.
5.3 x 4.1 x 1.1"   25

Flaco Ghost IV (*The Owl of Minerva Takes Wing Only at Dusk.*) Assemblage with imprint on plastic sheet, paper cutout, and metal object.
6.5 x 4.4 x 0.9"   30

Not Every Window is a Door. Assemblage with plastic sheets and print.
5.4 x 4.3 x 0.75"   33

On the Nature of Things. Assemblage with paper cutout, metal pole, and rodent bones from Flaco's digested prey. 7.6 x 5.5 x 1.5"   38

Flaco VII (*And the Lion Shall Lie Down with the Lamb.*) Assemblage with paper cutouts, rusted object, and wood. 6.1 x 4.75 x 1.4"   41

Wagen der Rettung, Höhle mit Gebein. Assemblage with painted paper cutout, metal, rusted objects, and rodent bones from Flaco's digested prey.
6.1 x 4.75 x 1.4"   45

The Melancholy of Distance. Assemblage with paper cutout and rusted object.
5.54 x 4.25 x 0.4"   50

Flaco Ghost XI (*Flaco siderealis.*) NYC, 2024.

Acknowledgements

Funny how we strain to grasp reality, then find it only in suspect reveries.

Thanks to Heide Hatry, Simon Carr, Elizabeth Gray, Patricia Karetzky, James Sherry, James Thomas Stevens, Anselm Berrigan, Cleo Li-Schwartz and Zhang Er for helpful pointers along the way.

— Leonard

Thank you Leonard Schwartz, Tod Thilleman, and Flaco. Thank you, Eileen Ross for helping me to locate Flaco on any given day. Thank you Charlie Rudalavage for your dedicated work. Thank you, Stan Schnier for your advice and photographic expertice. Thank you, Alan Rosner, for your wonderful stuff. Thank you, Chris Ang, for your inspiring photos. Thank you Dan Wechsler, Adam Weinberger, Dave Bergman, and John Wronoski, for helping me to find books to alter, and John Wronoski and Laura Hatry for always being there for me.

— Heide

Bios

Leonard Schwartz is the author of numerous books of poetry, including, most recently, *Actualities I: Transparent, to the Stone, Actualities II/III: Two Burned Hotels,* and *Actualities IV/V: Comic Earth* (2021, 2022, 2023, Goats & Compasses). His three books with artist Simon Carr, *Horse on Paper, Not a Snake,* and *Salamander: A Bestiary* (Chax Press, 2017), are also out and about.

Heide Hatry, is a NYC-based German artist, former rare bookseller, and best known for her work employing animal parts or other discarded, disdained, or "taboo" materials. She has curated numerous exhibitions and has shown her work at museums and galleries all over the world. She has produced hundreds of artist's books, edited dozens of art catalogues, and four of her larger projects (*Skin, Heads and Tales, Not a Rose*, and *Icons in Ash*) have been documented in monographic books.

.

www.ingramcontent.com/pod-product-compliance
Lightning Source LLC
Chambersburg PA
CBHW040852120626
46547CB00006B/574